J 634.772 ROB

Robson, Pam.

Banana /

4v 7/00 LT 5/00 CHAVEZ-J

D0899257

What's for lunch?

# Banana

Library of Congress Cataloging-in-Publication Data
Robson, Pam
   Banana / written by Pam Robson. -- 1st American ed.
   p.  cm. -- (What's for Lunch?)
   Includes index.
   Summary: Presents facts about the banana, including
where and how it is grown, harvested, and marketed, and what
other products are made from bananas.
   ISBN 0-516-20826-8
   1. Bananas--Juvenile litertaure.  2. Banana products--Juvenile
literature.  [1. Bananas.]  I. Title. II. Series: Robson, Pam.
What's for Lunch?
SB379.B2R65  1998                              97-6502
634'.772--dc21                                 CIP
                                               AC

© 1997 Franklin Watts
96 Leonard Street
London
EC2A 4RH

First American edition 1998 by
Frankin Watts
A Division of Grolier Publishing
Sherman Turnpike
Danbury, CT 06816

ISBN  0-516-20826-8 (lib. bdg.)
ISBN  0-516-26217-3 (pbk)

**Editor:** Samantha Armstrong
**Series designer:** Kirstie Billingham
**Designer:** Dalia Hartman
**Consultant:** Paul Barrett
**Reading Consultant:** Prue Goodwin, Reading and Language
Information Centre, Reading

Printed in Hong Kong

# What's for lunch?

# Banana

Pam Robson

CHILDREN'S PRESS®

A Division of Grolier Publishing

LONDON • NEW YORK • HONG KONG • SYDNEY
DANBURY, CONNECTICUT

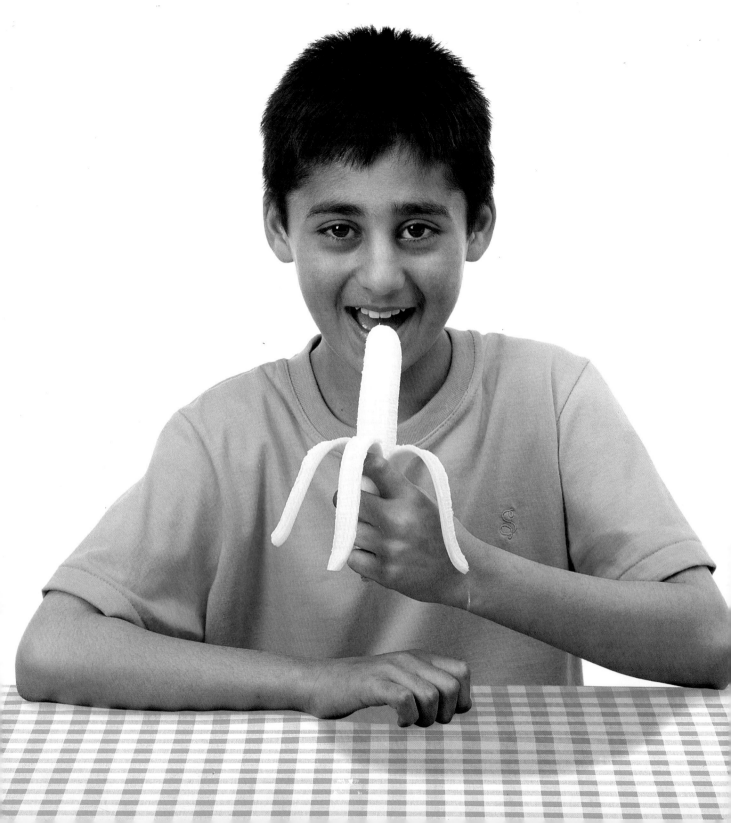

Today we are having a banana for lunch.
We eat bananas as a **fruit**,
but they are also used to flavor a lot of foods.
Bananas contain **vitamins**, **proteins**, and **fiber**.
Eating bananas will give you **energy**.

Bananas grow on plants.
The plants look like trees, but
instead of a trunk, they have
a stem made from leafstalks
rolled around each other.
One leaf can be big enough
to use as an umbrella!

Bananas grow in countries where the sun is always strong and where, for part of the year, there is also a lot of rain. Farmers in the West Indies grow bananas.

Their bananas are sometimes destroyed by strong windstorms called **hurricanes**.

The farmers grow their bananas among tall trees, to protect them from the wind.

Most of the bananas we buy
are grown on large farms
called **plantations**.

Sometimes **rain forests** are cut down to make room for the plantations. Many people think this is wrong because it destroys wildlife.

Some fruits like apples have
**seeds** called **pips** inside them.
When the pips are planted,
new apple trees grow.

Bananas do not grow from seeds. Instead, a **sucker** grows from the plant **root.** The sucker will become a new banana plant. The farmers put the new plant into the earth.

Farmers are always busy
looking after the growing plants.
They trim them so that
the bananas will have
room to grow.
They also check to make sure
there are no insects or diseases
on the plants.

Each plant grows one **stem**
with up to 200 bananas on it.
A large bunch of bananas is called
a **hand**, and each banana
is called a **finger**.
The bananas bend upward
toward the sun
and become curved.

The farmers cover the bananas
with special **sleeves**
to protect them from bad weather.

After a year, the bananas
are ready to be picked.
They are still green.
Each stem is cut off the plant
with a knife called a **machete**.
It takes two people to do this
as the stem is very heavy.
The bananas are hung from
moving cables that take them to
the packing station.

In the packing station the bananas are washed in large baths of cold water. The water also keeps the bananas cool. Bananas are easily damaged, so they are packed quickly and carefully into boxes.

The boxes of bananas are taken to special
ships that have cool compartments.

These keep the fruit fresh
on its long journey.

On arrival some bananas
are placed in special ripening centers.
There they are warmed until they ripen.
This means that they are still fresh
when we buy them.
Bananas are used
to flavor lots of things,
like milk shakes and yogurt.

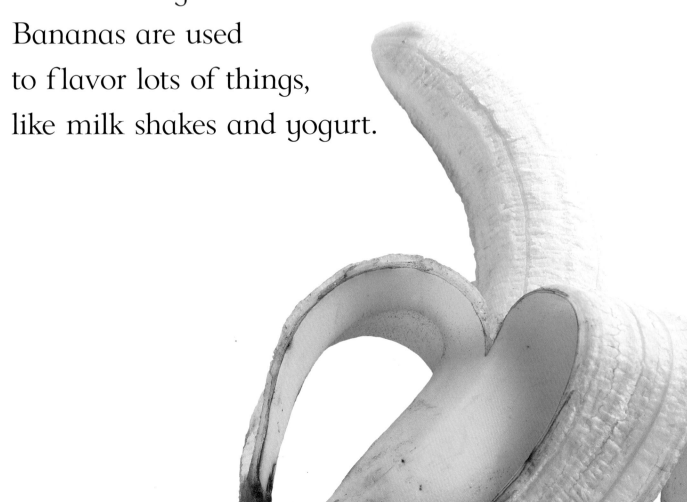

Bananas can be cooked.
They can be made into a pie
or a banana cake.
Sometimes bananas are dried
so that they last longer.
They can be eaten as a snack
or in breakfast cereal.

Some fresh fruits, like raspberries,
can only be found in our shops
at certain times of the year.
But bananas are always there.
They are delicious.

# Glossary

**energy**      the strength to work and play

**fiber**      something found in some foods
that helps you to digest what you eat

**finger**      a single banana growing in a bunch

**fruit**      a food that usually grows on a tree or a bush,
such as apples, oranges, or bananas

**hand**      a large bunch of bananas

**hurricane**      a storm with very strong winds

**machete**      a heavy knife with a wide blade that is
used to cut the thick banana stems

**plantation**      a large area of land that is used to grow one
kind of plant, such as coffee, tea, or bananas

**protein**      something found in foods like milk, cheese,
bananas, and meat that helps to build the
body and keep it healthy

**rain forest** thick forest found in the hot, rainy parts of the world. Many different animals live there.

**root** the part of a plant that grows downward into the soil and takes in goodness and water to help the plant grow

**seed** the part of a plant that grows into a new plant

**sleeves** plastic coverings with open ends that farmers put over the bananas to protect them against cold weather or rain

**stem** the part of a plant that supports the leaf, fruit, and flower

**sucker** a new shoot growing from the root of a banana plant

**vitamin** something that is found in fresh fruit and vegetables that keeps the body healthy

31

# Index

**Picture credits:** Bruce Coleman 7 (Peter Terry); Courtesy of Fyffes 13, 14, 20; NHPA 15 (Stephen Dalton); Panos Pictures 10-11 (Neil Cooper), 16 (Philip Wolmuth), 19 (Paul Smith), 22-3 (Paul Smith), 24-5 (Philip Wolmuth) Robert Harding 8 (G. Corrigan); Nick Bailey Photography cover, 3, 5. All other photographs Tim Ridley, Wells Street Studios, London. **With thanks to Ushil Patel and Edward Evans.**